Thinking of You

Also by Courtney Peppernell

Pillow Thoughts

Pillow Thoughts: Deluxe Edition

Pillow Thoughts II: Healing the Heart

Pillow Thoughts III: Mending the Mind

Pillow Thoughts IV: Stitching the Soul

Once Upon a Feeling:
A Pillow Thoughts Affirmations Deck

The Road Between

I Hope You Stay

The Space Between Us

Watering the Soul

The Way Back Home

Time Will Tell

A Month of Sundays

Out of the Ashes

The Last Poem: A Novel

Thinking of You

POEMS ON GRIEF, LOSS, AND HEALING

COURTNEY PEPPERNELL

Andrews McMeel
PUBLISHING®

Acknowledgments

Thank you to all those who worked on the creation of this book, from editing, design, and illustration to management and sales. So many long days and quiet hours went into bringing this to life, and I'm grateful for each hand that helped shaped it. Justin, Liz, Danys, Kirsty, and Diane: dream team! I can't thank you enough.

This book is about grief. The kind that takes many shapes: loss, change, heartbreak, distance. And in those moments, it matters deeply who you have around you. I'm thankful for my support network: for my friends and family who have been steady and kind; for my partner, who brings comfort in all the right moments; and for our dogs, Dakota, Benjamin, and Marlu, who are always the light on dark days.

This poetry book is a little different. It's based on the collection my character Wren writes in my novel *The Last Poem*—a book within a book, created for her grief group for which poetry became the way back for them all. Though Wren is fictional, her words, like so many of mine, were born from real moments of sadness and healing. There have been many moments in my life when grief left me wordless, and poetry gave those feelings a place to go. Wren and the grief group in *The Last Poem* (Henry, Olivia, Emerson, Winnie, Gill, Bobby, Julian, and Rita) reminded me that, even in loss, there is still art, still beauty, and still the chance to heal.

Thank you for reading.
Thank you for being here.

Come say hello . . .

Instagram: @courtneypeppernell
TikTok: @courtneypeppernell
Email: courtney@pepperbooks.org
www.peppernell.com

This book deals with grief and loss—
read with care.

Perhaps there was a point in time when your life became unsteady and you lost all the things important to you, before you were ever ready. In such grief and agony, you struggled to go on, to rise again through every moment and every haunting song. On the eve of all you thought you knew, a raven appeared and promised to guide you through. The raven sat with you for many moons, through all the darkness, despair, and gloom. Upon your journey, you buried your old life and mourned the things that could not be, and while the fury and bargaining challenged your ability to see, these were the things you had to feel along your path to finally be free.

And then, one day, a bluebird arrived at your door, reminding you that life could be lived again, and it would be more beautiful than ever before. The seasons changed, and so did you, finding a release and the determination to fly, knowing that, despite every circumstance, you would persist and uncover the courage to get by.

You must remember there is no pattern to the stages of grief; it comes in waves and challenges our resolve and belief. And yet to survive is to understand that the raven and bluebird go hand in hand, a dance of darkness and joy. For even in the moments when we feel our lives have been destroyed, and the light is nowhere to be seen, you must move forward. For even if what was is now gone, you will undoubtedly discover your strength to carry on.

Stages of Healing

If You're Here, This Is for You

Grief can be many things: death, illness, heartache, loss of belonging, loss of home, relationships, friendships or opportunities, loss of dreams and expectations. Whatever it may be, they all share something in common: the life you once knew is over and a new one has begun, whether you were ready for it or not. You were a square your whole life, or maybe an octagon, a circle, or a diamond, and suddenly life shifts, grief finds you, and you are changed. You are a square living as a circle, a bird living as a fish, a tree living as a shadow, a flame living as water. The essence of who you were is transformed, navigating a world that no longer fits the shape of your past.

Living with this new reality is messy. You must remember that healing is not linear, nor is it packaged neatly. There is no set time line or order for your healing; there are no levels to complete or stages to master or a strict schedule to follow. Some days you will climb the ladder, others you will only make it one or two rungs, and on some, the ladder will be crumpled on the floor. You can grieve long relationships and short relationships, someone you loved unconditionally, or someone you never even had. You can grieve fulfilled potential and unfulfilled life changes, even if they are positive. You can grieve the person you were, as well as the person you thought you'd be. You can grieve missed opportunities and changed expectations. Your grief can come and go and return. You can still find joy and laughter while grieving. You can think clearly, cloudily, or not at all. You can feel surrounded by love, alone, or somewhere in between—all at once. You can close the gap between you and your grief, only for it to resurface years later as though it just happened.

Grief ultimately weaves its way into the very seams of our souls and seeps into every aspect of our lives. Yet it also reminds us of our resilience during a delicate balance between holding and letting go. Grief lasts, but perhaps the reason for it is to remind us of our deep capacity to love. To go through grief is to find ways to live as a new shape.

For whatever reason you are here, I hope you find a friend through the pages, because even though grief is very much part of life, things needn't be grieved alone.

Use this space to tell the story of how you're still here. It can be to yourself, to the one you miss, to someone who loves you, or to grief itself.

Thinking of You

The Weight of Grief

Grief is the shadow love leaves behind,
an endless ache, a weight undefined.
It settles in places where memories grow,
in every goodbye we can't let go.

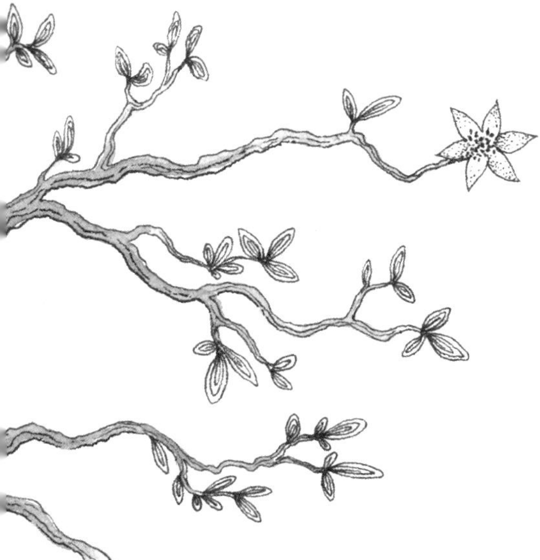

Believe me, I tried to bury it—
the truth.
Because I didn't want it to be so.
I tried to deny the ache, the suffering,
the hole in my heart.
But I could no more deny
the path laid out before me
than the sky could deny the sun in the morning.

It's the kind of dance that made you feel alive, but no one else knew the steps. One minute, they were all you could think about, and the next, they stopped answering your calls. It's not as though the thread was simply cut—it just frayed over time. Perhaps the most difficult of all was the almost love, the almost togetherness, the almost you and me. The ache does not subside overnight; it's not a feeling easily felt or a word easily spelled. There is no other way to describe "what-if." You will wonder how to say goodbye, what happens now when you exist outside of each other. You know where they keep their journals, and they know your favorite constellation, but you both went in another direction.

And the day has come and gone for the hundredth time that week, and you realize life has been disappearing right before your eyes. All life seems to do is keep moving even when you have felt stuck for all this time. Those memories piled into the corner of your room, sweaters and old cards and Polaroids—what to do with all those moments? To keep them or to bury them, to remember or to forget? The world never teaches you what heartbreak wants you to know: holding on makes you ache as much as letting go.

You are so far away now,
as though we are in different
lifetimes—
split between the stars.

I close my eyes
and find forever with you.

Every time I run into friends we used to share, they tell me it's been forever, even though it hasn't. The weeks have felt like days; the hours have felt like minutes. Time is moving in a way that makes me feel I will be hurting for the rest of time. I can't bring myself to make peanut butter sandwiches anymore, because they were your favorite, and we'd run to the kitchen at three in the morning to make two, sometimes three. I can't watch old movies without seeing your face in the screen. I still dream of the way you held me when it rained, but every time it rains now, I imagine every drop is another piece of me lost to the ache in my chest. I run and I run and I run, but I cannot escape the memory of you—it chases me through fields and city sleet and never lets me rest.

It is a process to learn
how to unlove you—
only there isn't a list
of instructions or a guide
on what to do;
instead, it is just your face,
your laugh, your voice
haunting me every time
I think of you.

The pieces will never
fit the same way;
the painting will look
a little different,
but it will still be beautiful
because you'll be happier.

I know that you still exist,
somewhere in the very depths
of my soul.

There is a softness to this place.

It holds my grief, and yet it is
filled with all the beautiful and silly
memories of you.

All the love lands here.

I have visited this place many times.

You still live here.

There are days when your name
is written in the stars,
and then there are days when
it is lost in them.

This is grief.

The life that I had always known ended. It was gone in an instant. One day, I went to sleep and my heart was still my heart, and then I awoke, and it irreversibly changed. An emptiness arrived that I had never expected, a fear that shattered the ground beneath me, pain that seemed to last for eternity. Here was a new road to walk, a new way to be, and I was so terrified that I would lose myself getting there. But that was the entire point—I was lost, changed, and unsure, but I was on my way to being found.

There were many things
I found after you were gone—
your favorite book, your watch
and necklace, too, all your clothes
and shoes, a birthday card
from years ago, coasters from
all the cities we had been to.

And yet the part of me I could not find
is who I was when I was with you.

You are gone, and I am too.

You were still with me,
even though you had left.

I saw you in the light as it
filtered through an open window;
I heard you in the sound of the sea
as it rolled over the shore;
I felt you every time I would come
home through the front door.

I could smell you in the seams of
all the sweaters I owned
and taste the memory of you in all
the meals I would eat alone.
How could my love for you still
be so alive when you were
no longer here?

Where do I lay my grief,
if not with you?

I buried myself that day.

The hopes, the dreams,
the expectations—
all of it had disappeared.

I spread rose petals over
the freshly thrown soil,
and I had a moment of silence
for the person I had been.

We are different now.

My gravestone read:
"She is changed."

And yet the sun still rose
beyond the hill.

There is light
in new beginnings.

Time moved forward for everyone, including me. And as such, it created more distance between the last time I saw your face, or held you, or heard your laugh. Every time the sun rises and I live another day, I have left you behind—it hardly seems fair—and life demands that I navigate the world without you. Here I am, rebuilding myself around the loss of you, and while perhaps it looks different, I still find you in the framework. Beautiful, isn't it? That I know grief because I have known love?

I think of the everyday ache like a flicker of a spark; it's always there, painful to touch, but does not engulf me. And then there is the ache through special seasons—holidays, birthdays, anniversaries—when that spark becomes a wildfire. It rips through my heart and soul and reminds me of all the ways I miss you, like when a song you loved plays unexpectedly, the smell of strawberry jam, or the way you used to pick at the frosting of your cake. But more often than not, it's a seat that shouldn't be empty.

You will know grief as though
it is a hand always on your shoulder,
yet you still have to wake up each day
and do the things that need doing,
and as such, grief will follow you.

It will be with you in all the mundane
moments, a cloud over the simplest tasks.

It will be there in the quiet, lingering
at the edges of your thoughts.

But you will also learn how to carry this grief—
how to honor such loss by continuing to live.

It felt as though I had been blindsided.
I was given an ache that I had not been
prepared for; grief found its way to me
at a time when I wasn't sure I could survive it.

And I had a dream of a tree standing tall,
every branch a stage of my healing.

The more I climbed, the more I felt the sun.

I have walked down memory lane
one thousand times,
for it is here that
I can see you, hear you, feel you.

And the hardest truth is that
this is where you live now—
but I can never stay.

There is grief that rearranges your soul. The kind of loss that brings about a shadow, so dark it rots all the flowers in your garden. An absence that breaks you every time you hear their name, emptiness that impacts the way you look at each day, a pain that lingers even as you laugh—a fragility that changes everything. And in such grief, you will come to know others who have been touched by this grief as well.

I hoped to make new skin,
one that would not pierce
or bruise so easily.

But what I learned was—
I will always bleed.

Something or someone cuts you,
and you always bleed.

But it heals, the skin regrows,
and you move on.

I look for you in the space between light and dark, hoping I might hear your voice between raindrops. I think of you in every sunrise, how I wish we could have spent more of them together. There are so many things I want to share with you, to ask your advice on. How can life go on without you here? Some days, a breath catches in my heart, and I pretend you have only stepped out of the room—but then the truth finds me again, and I am reminded you are gone, and I am still here. It breaks my heart, to live in a world where there isn't a *you*.

A dream dissolved into sorrow,
hopes unspoken and never known—
for a tiny heartbeat did not continue.
A love's echo lingers in its place,
where grief takes up so much space.

If we had one more day, I like to picture what we would do. Perhaps we would chase down the early dawn light as it rose over our favorite hill. We would wander through old forests, the soles of our feet crunching through leaves as we listened to the sounds of all the birds we saw. We would visit all our favorite places—the market by the dock, the lighthouse at the edge of the cliff, the ocean shoreline, the paved street with the colorful murals, the restaurant with the fairy lights strung from corner to corner, the bakery with almond croissants. One more day, and our conversations would be filled with laughter, every word filled with purpose and intent, mistakes forgiven, hearts a little bigger. That is just the thing; we always think we have tomorrow, until we don't.

Somehow the seconds kept ticking,
even though it felt as if time had stopped.
Days went by, and I took them hour by hour.
Months went by, and I took them day by day.
Until a year rolled into another one,
and I learned not to be afraid of the grief—
for while I was broken, I was still here.
Even if the grief never got any smaller,
I became stronger and stronger,
until I was able to carry it.

I thought that if
I chose not to heal,
then the door to you
would always be open.

This pain I carried for you
would forever keep you alive.

But you are not here today;
you will not be here tomorrow
or the days or years that follow.

You live in all the moments
that were before.

Even though I am no longer here, know that I am the sun rising above the hill. I am the wren perched upon your windowsill, I am the breeze that whispers through your hair, I am the pulse of your heartbeat, steady and always true. I am the stars in the night sky, a light guiding you when you feel lost. I am the warmth in every embrace, the quiet strength when you need it most. In every moment of joy and sorrow, I am with you today and with you tomorrow. You'll hear me in your laughter and feel me in your tears, for I will be with you, through all of your years. Once I was, and now I shall always be, in your heart and in your mind, a part of you, forever intertwined.

There will be a time
when grief arrives on your doorstep—
it will demand all that you are
and all that you've been,
to survive the ache is to live day by day,
step-by-step, believing in the hope
that tomorrow will be seen.

There will be days,
while floating in your grief,
when you'll wonder how to ever
move on from this—
even on the better days
that give you some relief,
there are some people
we'll always deeply miss.

You will bury many versions of yourself
throughout your life.

You will experience loss that feels as though
you will never live through it—
and yet you do.

And while you navigate such times,
there will be so much the pain teaches you
about your own worth.

You will be reshaped, finding courage in places
you'd long forgotten.

Loss is sewn into life.

It reminds you in every tear shed, and every
heartache felt, of the impact someone or something
had on your soul.

It is bittersweet;
to grieve deeply is to have loved deeply,
and such love, in every form, in every way,
is an honest measure of worth.

Living with Loss

If you have ever wondered
what your loss means to me,
it's a hole as vast as the sea,
the pause in my song,
a piece of my heart,
where you will always belong.

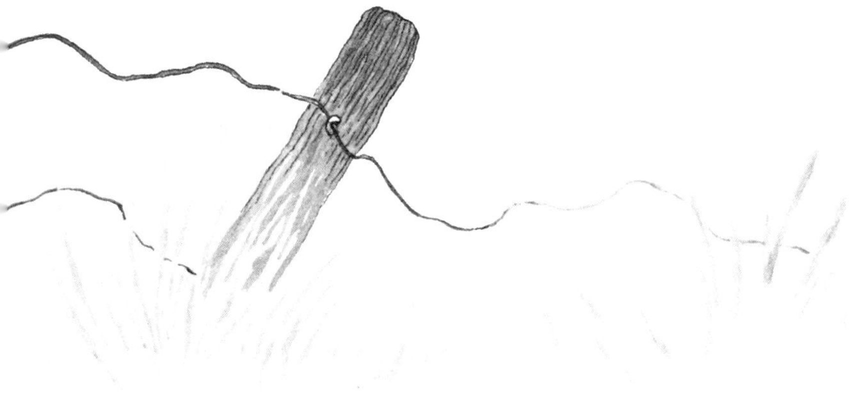

I felt alone while mourning. Every time I laughed, someone would say, "You must be feeling better." Every time I brushed my hair or left the house, someone would say, "Look how far you've come in moving on. Your smile is returning, there is plenty left in life to be grateful for, you will be stronger for living through this experience." So many platitudes, so many people wanting to cloak me in positivity. But this wasn't the support I needed. I didn't need to be ripped open in this way to know what made life so beautiful. This grief was anything, everything, all at once, little by little; it was the whole world. And to everyone else, the more time went on, the more they believed my grief was getting smaller. But it could be five minutes or twelve years; the grief would always feel like it just happened.

There are some betrayals in life that fundamentally change you—maybe its unfaithfulness in spite of your complete devotion, deceit after years of trust, false accusations or stolen ideas—and with it will come a howling, shrieking pit of pain in your heart.

In the aftermath, you will stumble through your days, barely getting dressed, doing ordinary things, like shopping for groceries, collecting the mail, taking out the trash, because these are all the things you are told to do, all the things you must keep doing to move through the ache. And while in life it is important to keep moving, it is also important to sit in that pit and acknowledge such pain. For it is visceral, it is now part of you, demanding validation. Once you understand that this pain is not something to overcome but rather to make room for, it becomes quieter.

They say a poet
writes best in the
midst of mourning—
is this what I am to become,
always surrounded by loss?
An ache that never ends?

Loss is never the same; it never looks the same, feels the same, or tastes the same. Perhaps there are similarities, like the same color of worn-out jeans, but those jeans will always look different depending on who is wearing them. Loss, no matter what it looks like or feels like, will move us through sadness, fear, anger, heartbreak, anxiety, confusion, and so much more. Moving through each part means facing isolation, shock, and the raw agony of grief. But living with loss is remembering. The little things that are part of our day remind us of what we have lost, and while painful at first, it's the way we make sure what once was isn't forgotten. Loss has a profound impact on time, for the further in time you go, the more it feels like everything fell apart only yesterday, and yet at the same time, it feels like a lifetime ago. It *is* a lifetime ago; you were entirely different before and after the loss.

When the day is done, and I am searching for tomorrow, I still hear you call my name. It drifts through the shadows, flooding my dreams with thoughts of you. And often I find myself thinking back. Did I thank you enough for everything you did, how you were always there for all the things I needed—help with the garden, or a broken tap, teaching me to drive, and driving me home from the bar, a shoulder to cry on, a warm hug after a bad day, a smile when it felt like the whole world was in my way? Did I pay enough attention to all the little things—your favorite mug, how you took your coffee, how you loved a ballgame and the ocean as far as the eye could see? Have I made you proud? I try to be the person you taught me to be, filled with kindness and hope, honesty and integrity. I hope you knew; I would do anything to tell you again just how much you meant to me.

The pain from the betrayal was one thing—so, too, was the way it broke a dam inside me. I was flooded with insecurities, resentment, distrust, humiliation, doubt, worthlessness, confusion, and sadness. And amid it all, I had to live with the loss of me. I suppose that was the most hurtful thing, the way someone else's choices profoundly changed my life. It changed the way that I perceived love, the way that I walked through the world, and the way that I carried myself forward. People would tell me, "Everything will be fine in the end; you'll find yourself again." But the truth is, I am not here anymore. The person you once knew is long gone, forever changed. I am not the same, and I never will be again.

Grief is not a complete story. It is not a list to be checked off, with levels to climb or stages to complete. It is not a one-time event. But, instead, grief finds me in the places where it starts and ends, where endings turn into new beginnings, and somewhere in between. It lingers in the moonlight as it washes over your room; it lives in old photographs; it whispers in the quiet moments of dawn, when I first open my eyes and can swear you are still here. It hides in the scent of your favorite soap; it whispers through letters you once wrote and clings to the empty spaces where you once lived. It collapses in on me when I see or hear something that reminds me of you, and every moment when I look to the sky and wonder if you are looking down at me, perhaps we are looking at each other the way we used to. It is in the air, as though I am always just trying to breathe you in.

And then one day you were gone—
and I was filled with all the reminders
of you.

I found your scarf, and letters, books
and photographs, your toothbrush and
favorite sweater, and I put them all in a box.

You were everywhere and yet gone.

I desperately wondered what to do—
for if there was no trace of you, then surely
the grief would leave.

So I got rid of the box.
But I was wrong; the grief never left.

It stayed, and I wish I'd kept your sweater.

Things to Know While Grieving

There is no comparison in grief—you will grieve very differently from others.

Grief isn't just about feeling sad. You will feel many other things: anger, confusion, shock, numbness, loneliness, and fear. All of these things can coexist with feeling joy, happiness, and hopefulness. They are all normal.

There is no time line for grieving. You will always be dealing with some part of it. It is important to remember to go at your own pace.

Some people don't know how to talk about death, loss, or grief—but there are lots who do.

There are grief triggers—places, smells, songs, belongings that might bring back intense feelings of grief; it can happen anywhere and at any time. There is no shame in folding in on yourself after being reminded of your loss.

There are always moments to say goodbye, even if they are not physically here anymore.

You will feel regret. "I wish I had called more." You are allowed to feel these regrets, but don't let it ruin you.

There are no neat and tidy stages—it's all messy and confusing, one big giant scribble on a page.

Big life events, like holidays, anniversaries, and birthdays will be hard, but it is always the little moments that eat away at your heart.

You do not have to walk the path of grief alone.

Looking after yourself is a priority—grief is exhausting. You take care of yourself by eating well, resting, finding comfort in things that bring you joy, no matter how small.

Memories are comforting and painful at the same time; you can feel both.

To feel joy or to laugh is not to dishonor your grief; they are reminders of your resilience and your ability to continue to love and live.

You will feel lost, directionless, and unsure of what lies ahead. It is the hardest battle, not knowing what road to take and feeling fearful of the wrong one. There is no right or wrong road; it is just a road, and life is lived by continuing to walk it.

Nothing is simple about grief. Your life has changed. Your perspectives and your priorities shift. It is natural to grow through your grief.

Grief is a journey that has no end. Your healing will be an ongoing process. It is not about reaching a point where your grief is "over" but rather learning how to live with your loss.

There are many things in life that cause us to feel as though we are falling apart. There is a long list—losing someone we love, illness, relationship problems, death, uncertainty, stress—and there is no use in trying to talk ourselves out of grief, because it will always find us. In an ideal world, we would set aside the time to deal with grief, to walk alongside it, feel it, go through it, until we are ready to face the demands of everyday life again. But that is not life. Life is more demanding than this. There are people who depend on us, things that need doing; the world does not stop, even while we are grieving. Life goes on, even if loss takes up so much of our own.

So, when you find yourself cracking, breaking, splitting apart, ask yourself, *What helps hold me together?* Maybe it's walking or knitting or journaling. Maybe it's art or music, poetry or reading, rock climbing or swimming. Maybe it's support groups or therapy, compassion, or small goals. Whatever it may be, it is just like glue, and it will help to hold you together.

I am sorry that I don't have anything
better to say than "I am sorry."

Loss is not light and fluffy, it's hard
and prickly and rips us open.

There are so many things that vanish
when we lose something or someone
we love.

It is the kind of pain that, no matter
which way you look at it, still just
inevitably hurts like hell.

Your grief is not a sprint or even a
marathon; it's a race that goes on forever.
You just need to learn how to pace yourself
so that you can keep breathing.

You need someone who sees your grief,
who whispers, "Yes, this is horrible.
No, this isn't fair. Yes, this feels like
the world is ending—because your whole
life has been irreversibly shattered."

When someone simply holds your pain,
without offering a hundred different fixes,
the air feels lighter and just a little bit clearer.
Not because they've patched you up
but because they've acknowledged a truth—
"You've been blown wide open; it's okay."

The life I thought I had was vaporized, burned to the ground, destroyed. Who I was then is now gone, erased; she disappeared the moment it was all over, without a trace. Even if there were signs, it still came as a surprise. Everything has changed, and I find myself trying to hold on to the things that feel the same. The world I had now seems so far away, replaced by shadows, cold and gray. I searched for anchors, something honest and true, just to keep the ground beneath me too. I buried grief in work and care; for most days, it felt far too heavy to bear. But my grief was patient; it waited, and it found a way. Isn't it ironic that anguish arrives, no matter what you do or say? I dug a hole, lowered my soul, and covered it in dirt, but despite my resistance, always so eager to fight, grief still grew with all its might. Breaking through the earth, it's clear, it would always demand I face the fear. For if I was to find a new way to begin, I had to accept and let grief in. Don't you see? Loss is now a part of me.

The agonizing thing about loss is not the ache that I feel but what happens after the ache has settled. When I have picked myself back up off the floor, dusted myself off, and willed myself forward, what then? When life continues to unfold all around me, I am afraid the day will come when I will have forgotten what it meant to love you.

As these days stretch into weeks and the weeks into months, I fear the memories that once burned so brightly in my mind will fade. As I grow older, and time wears on, will the vision of your face, the sound of your voice, the feeling of your hand in mine, dwindle like the last embers of a dying fire? The way I loved you was my favorite story. How could I possibly forget all the lines?

To forget is to lose all over again. Perhaps the cruelest part of grief is the way it forces us to let go, bit by bit, until we are left with mere fragments of what once was. An exhausting paradox: I hold on to hope that the pain will fade and I will breathe again, but I dread the moment it does, for it will fade the brightness of you.

I dreamed of us last night;
we were in your car—
parked by our favorite spot.
We were talking like we used to,
in soft voices, a gentle love.

And then I awoke,
to silence and shadows.
Because you were not here.

I just miss the way we talked.

I Feared Forgetting You

The fear wrapped itself around me and refused to let go for so long. The fear of being alone, the fear of everything changing, the fear of starting over. But it was the fear of forgetting that haunted me the most; like a dark and unrelenting night, it was always there. It was quiet, and persistent, gnawing at the edges of my thoughts. I was terrified that all the little details would begin to fade away, slip through my thoughts like water through my fingers. The sound of your voice, the curve of your smile, the way your eyes lit up every time you laughed. I clung to every remnant of you, desperate to keep you alive in my mind. I replayed conversations in my head and moments we shared, as if, by doing so, I could preserve them forever. I kept photographs and letters, your hat, and your sweater; I kept text messages and voice mails, all to anchor you to me. For if you were anchored to me, you were still alive in the world. But time was relentless, and memories, no matter how precious, are fragile things. The fear wasn't just about losing those wonderful memories; it was that by losing them, I would lose you all over again. It was as though forgetting even a single detail would be a betrayal, a final act of letting you go. How would I ever be ready for that?

The loss brought all kinds of feelings, but it was the fragility that I struggled with. Because I knew that I was strong and resilient. I had always been someone who chose to move the branches off the road rather than sit and do nothing. But in those bleak moments, after my heart had been blown to bits, I wondered if perhaps I would never be able to move the branches again. I had felt weak, insignificant, and lost. Everything had been falling apart for months, maybe years, maybe the whole time. Perhaps the saddest thing, aside from your cruelty, aside from your inability to take accountability, aside from your sheer disregard for empathy or respect, was the worthlessness I felt in the process. How is it that we allow others to break us down, piece by piece? It took what seemed a lifetime to convince myself I was still capable of moving the branches from the road. I am beyond you now; if you called out my name, I would not hear you. If you appeared in front of me, I would not recognize you.

—you are nothing but a bad memory

If only I had five more minutes with you, this is what I would say: Every day, I am between two worlds—the one where you are here, beautifully vibrant, and full of life, and the other where I'm left behind, holding on to the thought of you, which feels more and more distant with every passing day. It is the most painful in-between, remembering and forgetting. It is almost as unbearable as living without you. But in this in-between, I also find clarity. Even if there are small details that fade, it doesn't diminish the love I have for you. Time cannot erase all the ways you have shaped my life. You live on in the way I see the world, the choices I make, and in the love that remains in my heart. And perhaps that is the most honest way to remember you: not in the details that might fade but in the impact you have had on my soul, which stays forever. Losing the people who impact us most is a loss that never fades. We'll always miss them deeply.

In the quietest parts of the night, I hear your voice,
whispers sent softly with the glow of the moon,
and my heart holds on, like it never had the choice.
That day, a star lost its light, gone far too soon.

And for now, I will see you in the morning sun
and in the lyrics of all the songs we've ever sung,
in the moments we built and the life we shared,
the warmth of your smile and how much you
 cared.

In the pages of our story, there's a hollow place,
a chapter left unwritten, an entire empty space.
But I'll fill it with our memories, line by line—
a reminder of our love, which stands the test of
 time.

I'll carry you with me, through the days and nights,
in every shadow, which eventually turns to light.
Though the world keeps turning, and time moves
 on,
I feel your love around me, and it holds me strong.

Do you hear me, in the autumn breeze?
I am the rustling of the golden leaves.
In the quiet moments when you feel alone,
I'm right here; you're never on your own.

In the warmth of the sun upon your face,
in the summer rain's soft embrace,
I am the whisper in the evening light,
holding you through the darkest night.

When you see the stars, and how they shine,
know that my love transcends all of time,
in every memory you hold close and dear,
I am right beside you and always near.

When your heart feels heavy and torn,
remember, my life is not for you to mourn.
Still I live on within you, strong and true;
I am a part of every little thing you do.

I want you to keep going and carrying on,
for my spirit is still here, never really gone;
in the folds of the life we once knew,
my darling, I'll always be watching over you.

I wish there was an end to grief. A note that says, "You went through the list: the crying every morning for a month, the sleepless nights, the avoiding people and places, and the endless replaying of shared moments. You checked them all off, so it's over now. One more week to go, and then you will never have to collapse at the sound of their name, or crumble when finding a lost sock in the laundry, or feel the weight of the universe crushing the life out of you, because you washed the pillowcase and it doesn't smell like them anymore. Your heart won't break because you needed to pack away their things, or close their accounts, or delete their voice mails, or cancel their subscriptions." But there isn't. Life ends, but death goes on forever.

The tears that have
fallen in your name
could be worth weeks
and weeks of rain—
and yet I still weep for you.

Navigating the hole you left behind
was like trying to find my way
with a broken compass.

The path is unpaved, the road filled
with carnage, an uncharted map.

And I knew all those who loved me
couldn't bear to see me hurting;
they wanted to fix the hole in my heart,
to take the pain away.

They wanted to carry it for me.

But it was not their burden to bear;
it was mine, and by carrying such a burden,
I learned to survive.

I mourned the person I had been before everything fell apart. I mourned that life, everything I thought it would be. It was gone. The plans had changed. The expectations completely washed away. And while I knew that I would never be the same again, I also wanted to honor the old me, for it was what she deserved.

So, I got up every day, I took a breath, and I started another day as the new me. I honored the old me by choosing to laugh again, by choosing to open my heart again, by taking things day by day, step-by-step. I honored the old me by reevaluating the people in my life, being grateful for those who lifted me up and removing those who didn't. I honored the old me by doing new things, listening to new music, walking more, dancing more, taking chances. I honored the old me by not being afraid to tell my story. I honored the old me by embracing the new me.

There are so many things I'd hoped to tell you—
how much I had loved carrying you,
how I had known you already, for you were mine,
all the dreams and plans I'd had for life with you.

But I never got the chance to tell you,
and you never got the chance to listen.
A little heartbeat I had held so close,
unexpectedly returned to the stars.

And even though I cannot hold you in my arms,
in my soul, I will tell you everything.

In your kitchen, time always stood still. With flour-dusted hands and a heart full of stories, you wove love into every dish, teaching us that food was more than energy; it was a language of the soul. Your garden, so bright and always blooming, was a reminder of how patient you always were; every leaf told a tale of care and nurturing, in the way you tended to gardenias and weeds alike. There, we learned life's beauty often hid in simplicity, and strength was found from gentle perseverance. Oh, your laughter, a song that could light up every room; it painted our childhood and lives in all our dreams. In every shared smile, warm hug, and cup of tea, you taught me of kindness and always just being me. Your eyes were windows to a boundless love, reflecting a lifetime of giving and forgiving, and in your soul, I saw our whole family. The threads that tie us were woven not in perfection but in the enduring acceptance of every lesson. Now, we gather to remember all that you were, and we promise to carry your love forward. Everything you taught us lives within our hearts. You are not gone, for you live on in us—in every act of kindness, every shared story, every time the sun rises and sets. You're here, embracing us, loving us still.

If I had known it would
all turn out this way,
that your heart would stop
while mine continued without you,
would I choose the same life?
And my answer is simple.
Even if I lived with grief each day,
I would choose you
in one hundred lifetimes.

Goodbye, Sweet Friend

The time arrived, the end of the road, a final call;
I can still hear your voice just down the hall.
All these long years, with your heart, so true,
this home just feels empty now, without you.

A wagging tail, a playful bark, and gentle ears,
you always knew how to calm all my fears.
With eyes that spoke what words could not,
you reminded me of joy, in the times I forgot.

Now silence wraps the space you filled,
the moments we shared, forever stilled,
but in my heart, your light stays,
a spark that guides my darkest days.

I hope you are running free, in fields of green.
In dreams and memories, you're always seen,
until one day we meet at the rainbow's end.
Goodbye, but never gone, my sweet best friend.

The little and unexpected things will always find you and break you open—a smell, a song, a memory. By knowing such loss, we realize that we are always grieving things; time passing, people leaving, goals half finished, unfulfilled dreams, opportunities we let sail by. But perhaps the only way to live is to know grief will live with us, to remind us that it is just a continuation of love. And if ever Hope existed on the horizon, it would say this: "Love was here first."

The firsts were difficult—the first breath after yours had stopped. It felt like I had sucked all the air out of the room. The first morning I realized it hadn't been a dream. The first letter that arrived in the mail, addressed to you. The first phone call, asking after you. The first time I stood in the grocery store, staring at mince pies, because they were your favorite, and you had no need for them anymore. I sobbed right there and then. And, of course, the heavy firsts. The first Thanksgiving without you, the first birthday, the first anniversary. They were all soul crushing, but nobody warned me about the seconds. During the firsts, people expected me to struggle. But by the time the seconds rolled around, those same people thought such time would be enough. There will never be enough time to close the hole in my life after you; I will always miss you.

—loss is infinite

In learning to live with the loss, there were so many things I mourned. So much of this time, I also mourned the fragility of life. How one day, everything could be completely normal, and the next, it had changed. One second, everything was the same as it had always been, and the next, I didn't even recognize my own life. I mourned every little moment that slipped away unnoticed, those ordinary days that now seemed extraordinary in their simplicity. I grieved for the moments that would never come to pass, the conversations left unfinished, the future that had been ripped away from me. How could it be that I had built a life and all these routines, and in an instant, it all crumbled, and the same routines now felt unfamiliar, hollow, and empty? I was left to try and piece together a new existence from fragments of the old.

But despite such upheaval, there was a rhythm to it all—a small voice that demanded I keep moving, even when it felt impossible. I know that life is not constant, how quickly everything can change, how fragile everything is. But I also know that our resilience is constant—bravery, too—and there is just something about love that will always pull us through.

You will be the flower
my garden remembers.
The loss will never disappear,
but I will grow around it.

The Fury Within

Grief is the ache that learns your name;
fury, the fire that fans the flame.
A storm beneath the mourning skin—
love, undone, turned wild within.

If there was anything
I learned from my grief,
it was that it had many faces.

The face I most feared was anger,
for she ripped and clawed at my soul—
the days were long and onerous;
the nights were even worse.

Until such time I learned
that underneath all the anger
was really just more grief.

Oh, I was so angry when you died. I cursed the universe for taking you away. I screamed at the night sky to bring you back. I questioned everything—*Why you? Why now? Why at all?* The silence was deafening; it offered me no comfort and no clarity. My anger at the world was a tangled knot of grief and love, intertwined so tightly that I couldn't separate one from the other. When you love someone or something so deeply, and then you lose them, it is the kind of anger that feels justified. *How could life do this to me?* Over time, the anger simmered, its sharp edges softened by the passing days. But the piece that was you will always be missing. This isn't to say the picture can't be beautiful—but without that piece, the jigsaw remains incomplete.

You were here, and suddenly you were gone.
My mind stumbles, my heartstrings fray,
broken by the relentless certainty of life.
Please tell me, why couldn't you stay?

Heartache pulses through my veins,
a nightmare I cannot seem to tame.
Lost in a darkened forest of sadness,
where every path looks the same.

I have tried to seek answers in the stars,
but they blink back indifferent and cold.
And in all this mess of loss, hurt, and fury,
only time can heal such ache, or so I'm told.

An illusion, it was—this great love you spoke of. It was not a great love, for it wasn't even real love. You were a liar, a cheat, a wolf in sheep's clothing. The image I had of you was false; I had devoted myself to a person who had been wearing a mask the whole time. And when the mask cracked, I took an axe and shattered the image I had of you into a thousand tiny pieces. The space it left behind filled with anger; it felt like it took up every inch of me. There were so many unanswered questions: *How could you betray me like this? Why would you humiliate me in this way? How could you be so deceitful to someone who had only ever been loyal and devoted?* But the anger taught me things I needed to learn. It taught me self-respect, to accept nothing less than honesty, to recognize the red flags, to pay more attention to someone's actions rather than the words they wielded. And in the end, I thanked my anger.

There are many things that knock the wind right out of your lungs—death; cheating partners; having a dream right there in your hands, only for it to be snatched away; things not going to plan; deep, dark days; losing someone, something, or someplace that you have tried so hard to love, work for, or strive toward. Those things will always feel unbalanced, unfair, and not quite right. It's a hard truth to swallow, that the reality of life is that it is not a fairy tale. You search for ways to cope, to continue getting up, day by day, and facing this reality. And the truth is, being optimistic isn't always sugarcoated mantras or glassy-eyed hopeless romantics—it's the grit and grind of choosing to face life, despite how difficult it can be. It's the choice to arrive at the battle and forge ahead. Real life isn't just stolen glances under moonlight, holding hands, and watching boats sail by. Real life is raw and gritty; it's tears and scars and bruises; it's heartache and anxiety, loss and grief, and moments of utter despair and frustration. It's about navigating the ups and downs, enduring the pain and challenges, shaping yourself through every experience, no matter how joyous or brutal, as you move through life on your way to becoming who you're meant to be.

My heart is surrounded by walls,
silent witnesses to my steady pain.
My soul a battlefield of sorrow,
raging against the endless rain.

But in the grief, a seed of hope,
sprouting love and light tomorrow,
tiny, fragile, but it's always there—
like a floating feather in the air.

I cannot think of you
without thinking of the loss;
it has shattered all I knew
and left me at a cross.

Tell me, which way do I go now,
as I gather pieces from the floor,
still grappling with the why and how,
wondering if I'll be whole once more?

Yet—

through the tears and endless nights,
and in all the mess and the pain,
I find fragments of you burning bright,
so that I may never forget your name.

It was overwhelming to feel such anger and be so mad at life. When the person you love deceives you in such a horrible way—the cheating, the lying, the emotional abuse, the extortion, the main-character syndrome—it is painful, brutal, upsetting, and utterly infuriating. It felt like nobody around me understood my anger. And how could they? They had not lived my story nor suffered in the way that I had. They had not experienced this level of deceit. It did not matter how many platitudes I heard; it felt as though there were no silver linings. And truthfully, sometimes there aren't. But it was the anger that convinced me to connect with others who did share similar stories. It was the anger that forced me to speak, to acknowledge the hurt that had been laid at my door. Through that anger, I found solidarity, and in that solidarity, I found strength. I realized that my pain, even though it was mine, was also part of a great human experience. The anger that once isolated me became a bridge to others who also understood the weight of such betrayal. In the end, it wasn't about finding silver linings; it was about finding the courage to go on, even when I was convinced I couldn't.

And you will see their anger
when you finally tell them no—
but the strength it takes
to stand your ground
is far more important than
their inability to understand.

I lived with anger for so long. Even on the days when I could laugh and feel the warmth of the sun on my skin, the anger was always there, like a silent storm, brewing beneath the surface. The waters were calm to the eyes along the shoreline, but the reefs below knew better; they knew the grief had turned into a relentless fury. Fate had cheated me, the universe had betrayed me, all that I'd hoped for had slipped away, leaving behind only anger, and that anger had questions: *Why now? Why me? What did I do to deserve this?* The injustice of it all burned hotter and hotter with every passing day. To navigate this storm, I had to acknowledge the anger. For denying anger a voice only gives it more power. The way through the storm was understanding that there was nothing wrong or abnormal about being angry, and I was allowed to take my time in moving through it.

There were so many moments when I was so mad for the person I had been—she had not known better; she was naive, too trusting. She did not notice the red flags; she buried the signs and her own feelings at the expense of another. She was afraid they would leave, so she sat with the abusive treatment. She was afraid of being alone, so she allowed them to walk all over her, even though she knew something wasn't right, even though she believed she deserved better. She ignored all her deepest, most-rooted instincts. All in the name of this so-called love. And that person knew this. They wielded manipulation like a weapon. They lied, belittled, gaslit an entire existence. How many times did she see something, only to be convinced otherwise? How many things happened that she knew to be true, but they gaslit her into thinking she was wrong, that she was to blame? This kind of realization tainted every memory I had. But the anger for the person who had been mistreated helped me to shape the new version of myself. This version stood her ground. This version said, "No more." This version held her head up high and said to the devil she had married, "You have no power here anymore. Your words are useless, your existence nothing more than a speck of dirt on a windshield I wiped clean." This version said, "I have found love for myself, and it is a shield that you cannot break."

It took me so long to speak about
the anger.
It was a vengeful darkness inside me,
and I could not seem to let it go.

Because the unfairness had no justice.
I had been tricked, conned, scammed,
all of it.

You played your part so perfectly,
a mask of kindness, soft and sweet.
But underneath, all a lie, cold as stone—
you are the worst person I have ever known.

It breaks you, this terrifying realization,
how easily someone can betray you.

I should have seen it sooner;
I should have.

I Don't Want to Be Angry Anymore

There are days when I mix up pieces of before,
like undated photographs in an ocean of
memories that drown my thoughts.

I am not sure where the sadness ends
and the anger begins; they are blurred
together, in a dizzy mess of hurt.

I was so afraid of losing you, and then
I was so afraid of losing myself,
and now I am afraid of the raw anger.
It is ruthless, warranted, and unmatched,
but it turns me into someone I do not
recognize. I feel like I am losing control.

And I don't have the words anymore
to describe or explain your selfishness—
it's beyond anything I can comprehend.

Tonight, I am hoping the anger will leave,
for it is the one and only hold you still have.
You are gone from my life now,
from my heart and from my soul.
Soon, you will only be a rotten memory.

Your anger will feel like a fire within, consuming everything and anything in its path. There is a fierceness to anger, a deepness in your soul, that leaves you feeling out of control. It will come and go. Sometimes, you will wake up feeling angry, and you won't understand why. Sometimes, things that don't normally frustrate you will spark and turn into a raging inferno. This fire will burn through your mind, your heart, and your soul, leaving behind a trail of scorched feelings. You will lash out, you will retreat, and you will repeat, repeat, repeat. But as fierce as that fire is, it is not invincible. It can be tamed, though not by denying its power. It is tamed by confronting and understanding the pain that fuels it. Anger is often a mask for our deeper wounds—loss, hurt, fear, grief—and in truth, they don't want to be fought; they just want to be heard.

I Spoke with Death

In the stillness of a moonlit night, I found myself wandering the stretch of beach near my home. The shadows danced under a silver glow as the sound of the waves crashed along the shoreline. My heart was heavy, an ache that had settled in since the day you left. Tired of walking, of feeling, of hurting, I sat on a weathered bench, staring into the dark abyss of the ocean, wondering how anyone was meant to survive such loss. I felt a shift in the air, and suddenly I was not alone. Death sat beside me.

"Have you come for me?" I asked.

"No," Death replied.

"Then why are you here?"

"I am here because you have called for me, even though you may not have realized it. Your heart is heavy with anger. I am here to offer you peace."

"Peace?" I scoffed. "How can you offer me peace when you have taken so much from me?"

Death's expression softened. "I understand your pain. Loss is one of life's most difficult challenges. It brings with it so many emotions—grief, confusion, anger—and they fill your heart."

"But this rage is burning a hole inside me," I said. "Why?"

"Anger," Death explained, "is a shield, a way to protect yourself from the raw, unbearable pain of loss. It gives you a reason to fight, a sense of control in an otherwise uncontrollable situation. It is sometimes easier to be angry than to open your arms to sorrow and grief."

The stars dotted the horizon like tiny sparks, as the weight of Death's words hung around us.

"What do I do with all this anger? How do I let it go?"

"First, you acknowledge Anger. You let it know that it is valid, that you have accepted the reasons it is with you. You cry when you need to, you scream if it helps, but you stand your ground and do not let the fury consume you. It is not your enemy, merely a companion on your journey."

"And then what?" I whispered.

"Then," Death continued, "you find ways to honor what once was. You celebrate the life that was had, the love that was given, the lessons that were taught."

"And then does the anger leave?"

"All that grief is never truly leaves us," Death replied. "It becomes a part of who we are; it shapes us in ways we may not always understand. But it also teaches us that between life and death is memory, and it connects us eternally."

When Death left, I sat on the beach for a long time, listening to the sea. I knew the road ahead would be long and difficult, but I also knew that I was not alone. Anger was with me, and so, too, Grief, and together they would remind me of Love, who, after all this time, is the reason for all things.

In the end, how dare you go and leave
when I still had so many things to say?
You took me for a fool, just a mockery,
turning love into ashes in my mouth.

There is a rage that boils beneath my skin,
a seething river of all that I was and had been,
everything you promised, broken by the void,
my whole life shattered and dreams destroyed.

It turned every memory into a painful shard,
cutting deeper and deeper with every thought.
Left me screaming at the sky in the backyard,
hoping the stars would swallow all this pain,
so that I may learn to breathe and live again.

You should place trust
in your anger,
for it is a voice for Love
when she cannot speak.

There will come a time in your life
when you will feel angry.
So angry, you'll be afraid it may consume you.

But it is how we manage anger that matters—
if acknowledged, understood, and channeled,
it can lead to growth, healing, and resolution.

Be with people who allow you to feel, express,
and process your emotions without judgment.

Suppressed anger is a pressure cooker;
it will explode one day.

The anger metastasized because I had always thought I'd have more moments. I had taken so much for granted, and I was mad at myself for that. I replayed every missed opportunity, every unspoken word, every time I chose something insignificant over something meaningful. I was furious at life for being so unpredictable, for ending what I thought was certain. It wasn't just the loss itself but the realization that I had lived always believing there would be more time, more chances, more tomorrows. The more I allowed the resentment, bitterness, guilt, and shame to build, the more it grew. Until suddenly the anger became a weight I carried everywhere. And it was heavy, suffocating; I could barely move through each day. And yet I couldn't seem to let it go. Because to release such anger meant admitting defeat—admitting that I had failed to appreciate the everyday little moments. But as life continued to unfold, I understood that holding on to anger wasn't going to change anything. It wouldn't bring back the love I had lost; it wouldn't erase what had already happened. The only way to release the anger was to forgive myself. Forgiveness, I learned, can be for many things, but mostly it is for ourselves, for being human—as messy and complicated as that is—so that, one day, we understand what matters most is not how much time we have but how meaningfully we use the time we're given.

The grief changed my life; it made me a different person. Undoubtedly, grief changes us—and within that deep, aching pain, I was also angry for all the time that had been lost. I believed I had wasted the best years of my life. I believed my chance at a happy ending had been eradicated, that I had lost too much time, that my opportunity for a family, success, and a beautiful life had been taken from me. And while it's true those years had been stolen from me, and I was allowed to be angry about this, it was also true that I still had all the same opportunities. For it is never too late. So, if you feel like you, too, have lost the best years of your life to darkness, I promise you, the best days are still ahead of you.

Endless What-Ifs

I rewrite the past in desperate threads,
endless what-ifs loud inside my head.
A deal with grief I cannot make—
as if regret could change the ache.

It felt like a lifetime of hard days. It was exhausting, the way the thoughts piled on top of each other like leaves falling in autumn, a tangled mess of color and decay. I cycled through all the what-ifs, a million ways it could have been different. My heart was splintered, and each time I tried to pick up the pieces, I'd cut my hands. Sometimes, it felt as though I'd never find the end of it, that I was destined to replay what could have, would have, should have been for all of time—that I would never understand the reason in the "why." As for myself, what I found instead was that the cards I had been dealt were unfortunate and unfair, but they were part of a larger deck. I would be dealt more cards, and I could turn them into a winning hand.

I had prepared to live without you, to know how to do that—I rehearsed the silence, so that the days without talking to you wouldn't feel as long. I memorized the places with all your things so that, when they became empty spaces, it would not feel as lonely. I told myself that time would dull the edges, that routines and distractions would fill the void. But what I had not prepared for was that, when you were gone, the world felt less bright, the days felt smaller. Living without you was an ache that stole pieces of me each day I rose in the morning. But perhaps the hardest part was knowing that you had so much more living to do. What would I have done differently, had I known the last goodbye would be the very last? Would I have held you longer? Would I have whispered the things I never had the courage to say? Would I have wished we had more time? I ask myself all the time, *What would I have done?* Maybe everything differently, maybe nothing at all, but I hope you knew how much I loved you.

You will never know if the outcome would have been different. The what-ifs will torture you. They will pervade your thoughts. You will replay scenarios over and over: *If only I had done this, if I hadn't done that, would this have happened? If these tiny moments hadn't happened, would the whole ending have been different? What if one variable were different? Just one little thing altered, maybe I would not be living with such heartache.* The world will tell you to stop doing this to yourself, that there is nothing you could have done to change anything. What happened has happened. But it won't stop you from running through your life like a playbook, overanalyzing small details, questioning every step you took. If only we could turn back time, but then again, what point would you turn back to? What would you change, if it meant all that you are now was undone?

And I lost count of all the days
I opened my eyes and thought—
How could this be?

I struggled to be the person
I had always been: openhearted,
trusting, calm.

Instead, I held on tighter,
I questioned everything more;
my hands always trembled
with fear, doubt, uncertainty—
the thought of starting life all over.

I seemingly folded myself in half,
wondering each and every day,
Was it all my fault?
Was I not good enough?
Was I nothing more than a crumpled
piece of paper to be tossed aside?

I wished I could rewrite those years;
I would have done it so differently.

But time machines do not exist,
and you cannot change the past.

The answers will come to you,
maybe not now, or tomorrow,
or the nows and tomorrows
that follow, but they will find you.

And it is true, if you look up,
the sky is always moving; so, too,
are the trees, the birds, the people,
everyone, everywhere, all around you.

But it is also true that, if you look
at your feet, the ground is steady
beneath you.

I have thought one hundred times,
Maybe the stars needed you more.
You were made to live in between
every beat of my aching heart,
just like you were always destined
to light up the sky.

It is a quiet ache,
the way we carry the burden
of what might have been—
we *almost* made it,
we *almost* fell in love,
we *almost* had it all.

The Grief of an Unlived Life

When we are young, we have endless hopes and dreams and are full of promise. Then, we grow, and the world around us changes, and sometimes dreams don't come true and hopes fade. We're left wondering how we are supposed to move forward when things have not turned out the way we wanted. There are many things that hold us back. What-ifs can be born from wishing we had made different choices; they live in between moments that are outside our control and things that alter the course of our lives. They make us believe that, *If only this had happened, or I had done this, then my life would be better—I would be happier, stronger, fulfilled.* Our gardens, once blooming and full of life, become frozen over. But perhaps that is the most rewarding thing about gardens: we can always plant new things. The landscape may look different, but that does not mean we cannot be happy, fulfilled, or strong, even while walking paths we did not expect.

A heartbeat once whispered,
so faint, so new,
a promise of life within—
now silenced.

Dreams wove themselves
into tiny clothes,
into names spoken softly,
into futures imagined.

Hands cradled a growing belly,
anticipation blooming with every kick,
every flutter,
a secret language between us.

Then, a quiet moment,
a shadow passed,
and the world tilted,
leaving emptiness behind.

Grief settles in the hollow spaces,
a presence of absence,
words unsaid, songs unsung,
a love that had no time to grow.

In the stillness, tears fall,
silent prayers to the stars,
for the one we never met
but forever hold.

Time moves forward,
relentless, indifferent,
yet in the quiet of night,
I feel you close,
a whisper of what might have been.

What if the road we didn't travel was
the one that would have forced us awake?
What if the words we didn't say
could have changed someone's day?

What if the chances we let pass
held moments that were meant to last?
What if the dreams we kept inside
were just stars waiting to collide?

Some people will tell you that, to live your life, you must wake up every morning without complaints, engross yourself in positivity, and be grateful without fault. And while there is merit to this—appreciation, positivity, and gratitude are all lovely things—to feel these things every single day is not rooted in reality. A day is not always good. Sometimes, it is terrible; sometimes, earth-shattering. Sometimes, it is wonderfully intoxicating. Sometimes, it is just ordinary. But whatever a day may be, we are not always able to control it. There are choices that aren't always the ones we would make; sometimes, we make mistakes; we get it wrong. You are allowed to wake up and feel guilt or anger, shame or regret. We are allowed to look at a day and think, *The only possible thing that I could do right now is just exist.* To feel the positive, to remember the appreciation, to see the gratitude, we have to listen to the disappointment.

Then I arrived at a point where I was sick and tired of people telling me, "But look what you have now." Because I already knew. As plain as the sky is blue, believe me, I knew. And I was still grateful for so many things—the warmth of the sun, the way my dogs looked at me, a beautiful night sky, the feeling of a well-walked hike, all the love I had in my life. But none of those things canceled out my loss.

By constantly telling someone to look on the bright side, to focus on the positives, to always find the silver lining, you are erasing their struggles, their sadness, their grief—you are invalidating how they feel. All unintentional, I am sure, but for your own benefit. Because seeing the people we love in pain causes pain.

To a hurt person, all you need to do is say this: "Yes, this sucks. Yes, this isn't fair. Yes, this feels like the end of the world. But if your world is burning, then I am right here, and I will be here, with you, beside you, for as long as you need me."

But how could you have known
what was going to happen?

Did you gaze into a crystal ball?
Did the tea leaves reveal the truth?
Did the stars whisper it to you in a dream?

How could you have possibly foreseen
it would end like this?

You couldn't—
and yet, you blame yourself anyway.

All of your what-ifs are what make the grief unstoppable, but if there is hope to be found, find it in the way those thoughts come for everyone who has experienced loss. You will take stock of every second, minute, and hour leading up to such loss, replaying events over and over—searching for anything you could have done to change the outcome. The loop goes on and on.

And the hardest part is that there is no magical solution. But there is compassion, and there is kindness, and there is patience; all of these things are what you need to show yourself.

And of course, it will be the most gut-wrenching, heartbreaking, soul-crushing thing you will ask yourself to do—to move on from the past and into the present and further into the future. Because someone you love is in the past. And even if that truth alone is enough to hold you back, one day, we all learn to understand just how much we carry them with us.

It was the fear that haunted me—
a giant mountain, one I thought
I would never climb.

One day, I stood in front of it.
I asked tentatively, "What if I fail?"
And the mountain replied steadily,
"Oh, but what if you succeed?"

In time, you will find strength
and meaning in the things
that seem unbearable,
but today is not that day.

Today is difficult and painful
and filled with regret.

It is anger and frustration,
immeasurable sadness and distress.

Today is not it.

But you know, some days just aren't.

The hope in all of this is that today
will end and tomorrow will arrive.

The Saddest List

It wasn't until I lost you
for the very last time
that I wished I had:
one more hug,
one more conversation,
one more "I love you."

If you had the chance to do it all again, would you? It's a timeless question, isn't it? What would you change if you knew you could redo everything? If you could go back in time and rewrite what was written? In the raw moments, the initial days and weeks, when it felt like I was splitting in half, I asked myself this all the time: *If I could erase the greatest grief of my life, and redo all those years, would I? If I could undo all the pain, and know what I now know, would I do it?*

And my answer now is no. I would live it again, because it taught me everything I needed to be who I am now—and that's something I wouldn't change.

After such an intimate relationship with pain, there is always going to be fear—fear of stepping outside your comfort zone, of letting yourself be vulnerable, of stepping out into the world again. And it will seem much easier to hide, to protect your heart, to run from the ache of disappointment, failure, or grief. But if you stay in the shadows, if you never take the chance on light once more, then you will miss the joy of connection. If you allow the fear to paralyze you, then you will watch your dreams slip away.

The greatest thing grief robs us of is not loss itself but of refusing to take chances after such loss. Because, when you avoid life, you miss the adventures, the surprises, the moments that will shape you into newer versions of yourself. Failing is not the ultimate cost; it is never taking the chance at all.

The Long Night

The night is a sea with no shore in sight,
and I am a lantern without the light.
Grief is the darkness, the wave, the air—
I breathe it in, and it's everywhere.

The night will feel endless,
a long stretch of darkness.

But each night, the sadness
will find you and show you
the depth of your love.

There was a whispered heartbeat once,
a quiet rhythm carried with hope,
a song whispered to the stars each night—
but the song slipped away.

So, too, did every promise,
of tiny hands that would hold yours,
the first breath, the warmth of life
growing within your own.

The silence fills every inch and corner
of your body, and of your heart.

The grief is a long and dark night—
for eyes you never looked into,
for a life you did not get to shape.
An ache for a future that never arrived,
to mourn the weight of what you lost
before it was ever fully known.

But still
you will carry the light with you
forever,
in the space that words cannot reach
in the moments between breaths,
where those promises will always exist.

It breaks my heart when I hear you say how lost you feel. When you call yourself ugly and unworthy, or that the weight of the world will never lift. When you speak as though you do not matter, as if you are nothing, it turns me inside out. I know how hard you are trying, to fight the demons inside. Because I see the wonder that you are, underneath all the reasons you try to convince yourself otherwise. I wish you could see the light that beats within you, instead of only knowing the dark. I know what it feels like, to have the hope dashed away. To be pulled under the tide, unable to follow the moonlight back home. But I know you'll make it out; the light will reappear eventually. I hope, one day, you will see it too. I know how hard that is—and until then, I will be right here.

You're right; the loss obliterated your life. The shock alone completely upended your day-to-day existence. The thought that your pain could one day turn into something beautiful is the last thing on your mind. Instead, you are grasping at straws, barely treading water, every moment a long, drawn-out breath. And we do want it all to end—the pain, the spiraling thoughts, the gaping hole in our hearts. Loss often leaves us with so many questions and so few answers. And, yes, you can rise again, you can love again, you can survive. But in the middle of such darkness, there is nothing beautiful about the hurt.

The sadness dragged me down to depths I had not understood before I had lived it. Someday, I had been told, I would know the pain of loss, and yet when that day arrived, it surprised me at just how long the day lasted. For it turned into weeks and years. My perspectives changed, my priorities changed—I changed. This grief was the heaviest weight I'd ever had to carry, and yet nobody could see it. It was an invisible thread pulling me back down the mountain every time I tried to climb it. As time passed, and I rose further and further up the mountain, despite the thread, people would say, "Look how much you survived the grief." Only what they didn't understand is that it was not only the grief I survived but each day. I have to survive this new way of living, because, every day, I am not the same as I was.

It's been so long since I lost you, and yet it feels like yesterday. All this time, navigating a world that suddenly felt tilted, like a picture frame hung just slightly askew. We were two sides of the same coin, and when you left, it felt like half of me vanished. The grief was an anchor, pulling me into depths I never knew existed, and for the longest time, I didn't know if I wanted to resurface. Grief has a way of making time elastic, stretching moments of despair into a forever, while compressing all the joy into fleeting snapshots. I avoided our favorite places and memories, hoping to dull the pain, yet this only drained the color from my life. But over time, I felt a shift—a sense of understanding. I knew that grief was teaching me a lesson. It was as though you were right there beside me. I knew then that I would always carry you with me—in the stories I told, the smile I had, the way I lived. The grief didn't have to be an anchor. It could be a bridge instead, to you, all that you were and all that I could be. Life moves forward and so do I. Your laughter plays in my mind, your strength gives me courage, your love reminds me I am never truly alone.

Grief never asks for permission;
it tumbles in, an unexpected deluge.

I see it in your eyes,
a long night that lingers,
an ache that words cannot touch.

If I could, I would lift it from you,
even just for a moment,
just so you could find a breath.

But all I have is this—
to be with you,
to carry the quiet with you,
to love you in the dark
spaces grief leaves behind.

And though I cannot fix what is broken,
I am here,
holding space
for all the raw pieces
you now carry.

You will grieve the path you were meant
to walk,
but I will walk beside you.

There is a gravity that
comes with grief.

It holds you in place—
a deep, starless night.

Until the stars return
and light the sky,
then you will hear the sound
of the heart that loved you.

The stars, you see, are proof—
the ones we love never leave.

To lose someone piece by piece,
little by little, is a soul-breaking journey.

Seeing grief in the distance, along the horizon,
and knowing it is coming your way,
you plead with it to slow down,
you ask grief to wait,
but grief waits for no one.

The world moves on, and yet you will still be sad inside, so sad that it runs through your veins and the air you exhale. There will be people who have forgotten your grief, who have expectations you are not ready to meet. When we say grief lasts forever, we mean you will always hold space for it. You will carry it with you, wherever you go; there is no escaping it. No matter how much you try to hide or how far you try to run, it is a shadow that never leaves. Some days, it will be small, a whisper in the back of your mind, a gentle tug at your heart. Other days, it will rise up, seeping into every part of you. People will demand things from you, as people do—smiles, conversations, time, energy—and you will give what you can, but the exhaustion will creep in. It will feel as though grief is completely taking over your space, as though there is simply not enough room for anything else. Yet you make room. There will be other things that filter in: joy, love, light, and laughter. Even as the grief remains. For it is in this very space that you find your strength.

The sky is never the same;
from one day to the next,
it changes—
colors and clouds, rain,
even the birds that fly by.

This is the same for our pain—
when we lose someone we love,
the pain never leaves,

it just changes.

I didn't understand the gravity of loss
until I had to say goodbye to you.

And it didn't matter if I tried to hold on,
because you just slipped right through.

I felt my heart sink that day,
like light fading from the sky.

We spoke of forever, plus one day,
but forever changed, and the sun lost its way;
now, it's just the quiet heartache of me
on the empty road, where love used to be.

There is distance between us now.
Only there are no calls or texts,
no letters or flights that I could catch
to meet you where you are.

You are somewhere I cannot follow.

And while it has been the hardest ache
in my life to be missing you,
if I have to miss you from here,
then I will also love you, so much so
that even the stars will feel it.

At times, the world feels too loud
for the hollowness of the ache inside.

In these quiet and fragile moments,
permit yourself to pause,
to let the sadness settle,
to give yourself the space to grieve.

And you will hear the whispers of healing—
I am here, in your stillness,
ready to listen,
ready to hold your hand,
ready to walk beside you,
as you learn to carry this loss.

In your own time,
in your own way.

It is not just you who I miss
but who I was
when you were still here.

The colors in the world
are different now;
each step feels heavier,
each night longer and longer.

Every word I say is more
thought out—
for what if it's my last?

I break for all the time
we had together
and all the time we didn't.

I am grieving you,
but I am grieving me too.

Maybe, in a different life,
we are still sitting at the
kitchen counter, and we
are laughing, drinking tea.

But today, it is just me, alone,
wondering how many tears
could fill this mug.

Before, I spoke of all
the things you are.
Now, I speak of all
the things you were.
Then, I talked of you
and smiled.
These days, I talk of you
and grieve.

And you make the best of it; you do.
You get up, and you find ways through.
But it is also true, there are so many days
you wish they were in your arms too.
Just to say, *I hope you know how much*
I miss you.

There is no moving on,
only forward.

And you carry them with you,
even if it's the space in your heart
that feels the most hollow.

For grief is only love,
with no one to follow.

There is not enough weight in "I'm sorry for your loss"—because I am also sorry that grief now sits at your table, uninvited, but here to stay. I am sorry that your heart aches in ways it never should, in places you didn't know could break. I am sorry that everything has changed and you were hardly given the chance to prepare. I am sorry that "goodbye" is no longer just a passing word but one that carries more baggage than anyone should ever have to hold. When I tell you how much your loss saddens me, what I mean is—"I'm here with love. Today, tomorrow, whenever you need reminding. For love, even though it changes, is never lost."

The sadness feels endless,
like it will swallow you whole—
yet you are still here,
breathing through the darkness.

The silent, relentless darkness.

Of course, surviving isn't grandiose.
Sometimes it's the quiet decision
to just hold on until morning.

The night lasts a long time, perhaps even forever. You may not ever be free of the grief, of the longest night, but you are also not defined by it. You can find all kinds of beautiful things in the night. There are stars, peppered across the sky like diamonds, a light to guide eyes across the sky. The moon, sometimes full, and sometimes just a sliver, but she is always there, changing and shifting, just as you do. There are fireflies, their soft glow proof that magic still dances in the quiet. Dreams are born in the dark, when your eyes are closed and possibilities are running through your mind. There is rest and reflection, where growth begins, tiny seeds that push through the soil, reaching for the surface. Yes, the night may last forever, but there is always the promise of dawn.

I need you to understand something: nothing is ever easy. I am sure you have been told one thousand times that everything will get better, that everything will go back to how it was, once you are past the hardest moments of your life. And there is truth to this; things will get better, and you will find a way forward. But hard moments will continue to happen. You will experience many more long nights. And I know that so much of the time it will feel like the world expects you to know exactly who you are, where you are headed, and who you want to be, but every once in a while, remind yourself that you'll spend a whole lifetime learning new things, evolving, and navigating.

You will always need a foundation to survive your grief. You will always need something or someone to lean on, to learn from, to understand that the real meaning of life doesn't exist in all the things we have but the memories we make and the dreams we hold on to. It is so easy to lose yourself in the folds of life, forgetting that the most precious things are often the threads of our everyday moments—good conversations, the laugh of someone you love, a warm hug, a sunny day spent outside, rain in the early morning, catching a shooting star. These are the delicate stitches that hold our lives together and remind us that, even in our deepest grief, life is still here.

Finding Serenity

Grief walks beside you, hand in hand,
but so does Hope—don't you understand?
The stars won't heal what's come undone,
but they'll guide you upward, toward the sun.

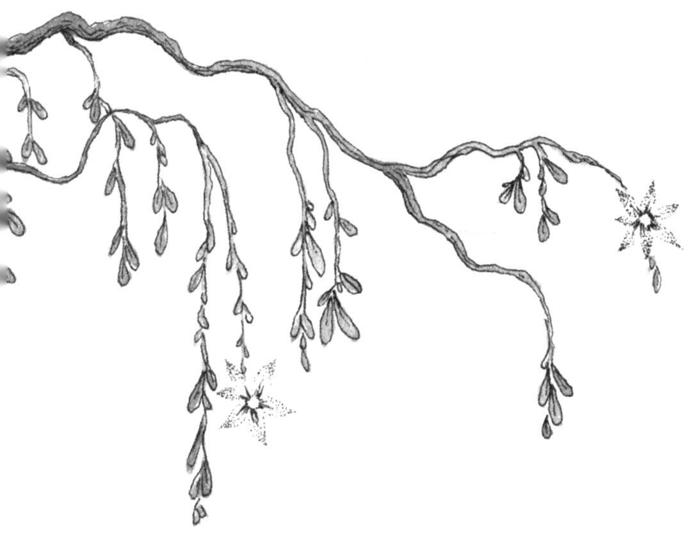

Serenity is the softness between heartbeats,
the breath that settles after letting go.

It's the warmth of sunlight on closed eyes,
a weight lifted, a gentle exhale after holding on,
a moment when nothing needs to be said.

It is not about eliminating
your heartache or never
speaking of them ever again.

It's about learning to live
with their memory.

Your heart is allowed to feel
this ache for the rest of time.

Whether it's five or twenty years,
or until your last breath—
someone you love is gone,
and it's okay to miss them
for the rest of your life.

I hope you carry faith
that you will survive
your grief.

That you will rebuild
and make things beautiful
once more.

That even though life changed,
and you cannot go back,
there is a way forward.

I hope you learn from your grief,
understand that even when
we make room for such darkness,
this doesn't mean the light
ceases to exist.

From both, new life can grow.

I didn't want life
not to have meaning
just because you had gone.
I wanted it to be full
of meaning for you.

I wanted every bright day
to be a tribute to how much
light your life gave to mine.

I wanted the little joyful things:
a cup of cocoa, butterflies
in the garden, a sun-filled day.
I wanted a reminder of you,
and every struggle, empty spaces,
old belongings, every memory
to be a reason to continue forward.

I wanted to carry on your dreams,
your laughter, your hope for better days.
I wanted the things you loved
to hold me together,
and the way I loved you
to be paths leading me somewhere new.

I wanted to make the world
as beautiful as you made life.

I still have conversations with you in my heart,
in quiet rooms, beneath the stars, after dark.

I ask you questions, and somehow
I find answers, in whispered words only I know.

It's not the same; it'll never be the same—
but I know you are still with me.

There are beautiful days filled with memory and messy days filled with tears, and on both I miss you. But in the most human moments—folding laundry, getting groceries, watering plants, waiting for changing seasons—I have learned to accept my grief. I cannot change what happened. It doesn't matter how many minutes or hours I have spent trying to reason with the universe, bargain with loss, or deny the inevitable; change does not mean what came to be but rather what will come to be hereafter.

The loss was earth-shattering, but the acceptance is an open hand. It is the letting go of the way you thought life should look and embracing how it unfolds. It's the deep inhale when the storm approaches and the exhale when it passes. It's learning to live in the gray, where some things will always remain unanswered. It's finding happiness in the middle of what you wanted and what you have. Letting go is not giving up—it's making space for all the things that you cannot change, on your way to becoming someone new because of them.

My grief is an entire garden,
and yet hope still blooms here.
Between the thorns and thickets,
in places I didn't expect.
New petals reach for the sunlight,
a reminder that in the most
heart-wrenching seasons of life,
you can still find your way back.

Looking at pictures of you no longer tears me to shreds. It still hurts, yes—it will always hurt—but my knees don't buckle beneath me every time I hear your name. Sometimes, I even catch myself laughing at a memory, letting it linger like colors behind my eyes. Words like "was" and "had been" don't taste so bitter anymore. They feel softer now, a gentle reminder of everything you gave me, everything you still are, even as the days count on without you.

—moving on

Time has moved on,
and the moments we
once shared are gone.

But light and love are
a part of every breath.
It is here I hold you;
nothing can divide us—
not even death.

Until we meet again,
I carry you in my heart,
I dream of you in my mind,
I feel you in my soul.

You will have always happened to me. I will have always met you, loved you, and eventually have been discarded by you. There is no amount of shame, embarrassment, anger, or grief that can ever change that. For the longest time, I believed the ending would be worse. There had never been any alternative, other than to persist. Because being alone was never an option. But your betrayal taught me new ways to love. Being alone was better. The ending of us revived me. It is the hardest lesson to accept that someone you once loved was never right for you, but when you get to the other side, you feel so much better.

Hope returned to me when I understood the difference between dismissive grief and accepting grief.

Dismissive grief can look like forcing yourself to stay positive all the time, letting those who have hurt you avoid accountability, burying yourself in distractions, convincing yourself to move on too quickly, silencing your pain, or trying to ignore your feelings.

Accepting grief, on the other hand, is allowing yourself to feel what you need to feel. It looks like giving space to your emotions, speaking about the hurt, freely and fully. It's setting boundaries and realizing that healing is a slow and gradual journey. It's understanding that grief is not something you can push away; it's asking yourself, *What do I need in this moment?* It's acknowledging that you can be both happy and sad at the time.

Then one day, I surrendered to the stillness your loss had brought me. I listened to the quiet, to all that I was feeling, and I began to sift through every thought. I am not controlled by grief anymore; instead, it moves through me, a current pulsating within my body. Though the loss of you was the greatest loss of my life, I understand that your love, your light, your presence was borrowed. You were here for a moment, and then it was time to go. But during your time, I felt your love, I felt your warmth, I felt happiness.

To know you was a gift.

The person you are missing
mattered.

They are still important,
despite not being here
anymore.

You find hope in continuing
to talk about them.

You can honor the person
you miss in many different ways—
by writing, or singing, or painting,
or talking about them or to them.

You honor them
by always remembering them.

You're twenty-one years old, and I hear you; the world is intimidating, and maybe you don't know how to love yourself. You're thirty-five years old, and life can feel a little jaded sometimes; there are truths you know, and they hurt. You're forty-three years old, and you wonder if you've done it all the right way; regrets are woven into your history, but maybe they don't have to define you. You're fifty-two years old, and you've faced heartbreak and hard days, but you're collecting small victories along the way. You will search for self-love at any age; it will come and go as easily as the tide. But always know, no matter how difficult the war you wage against yourself, love always returns.

I want to remind you of what it feels like to have purpose in every day. To rise in the morning without the heaviness in your heart. I want to remind you that you are allowed to be afraid of the unknown but that it does not need to hold you back. I want to remind you that you are capable of so many things, even if sometimes you second-guess yourself, your abilities, your strength. You start by believing in yourself, and then in love, life, and hope, and you promise to continue forward, even if there are strings that tether you to the past. They are reminders, wonderful memories, things that shaped you; they do not have to be anchors. I wanted to remind you that even if it took you so long to arrive here again, you still arrived, and you should be proud of that.

The road is often long and quiet.

It can feel as though you are waiting
forever for brighter days.

Those calm, safe, good feelings—
where are they?
Will they ever settle in my heart again?

It is so lonely.

Your life came to this standstill,
while the rest of the world kept moving.

And more often than not, it is not loud,
the way hope returns to us.

It is soft,
like finding a feather at the foot of the bed
and wondering if somehow it was left
by the one you love and miss.

It still hurts to think of you,
as much as it hurts
to not think of you at all.

This strange dance I find myself in—
I wanted to think of you always,
and then not at all.

If grief is anything, it is curious;
one day, I will think of you
and smile, and the next I will cry.

And then, somewhere in the middle,
I will find the in-between.

I will feel you here, a gentle light,
a warmth that stays, never gone.

And in this tender in-between,
I will uncover hope once more.

There's no "getting over it"—
just learning to live around it,
finding beautiful things where you can,
letting loss be part of you,
without letting it take over you.

Finding calmness and happiness again
means accepting that ache lingers.
It's choosing to always let love in,
despite the fear and the apprehension,
trusting that Joy can walk the same path
Grief paved out before you.

These days, I carry your memory,
not as a weight but as light.
The valley of grief once felt
so vast and endless,
but now I walk it gently,
with pockets full of purpose.
What was once so heavy
is now part of every step—
soft and steady, quiet warmth
that leads me home.

One day it just happens;
you wake up, and you are
in the place you have
longed to be in.

The one you have been
dreaming of for so long.

Your soul is calm, your heart
steady, your mind at peace.

You realize that perhaps
you don't need to understand
it all to make sense of every loss.

Sometimes accepting means
letting the questions be
and allowing life to answer
in its own time.

To find peace meant I had to stop using distractions to bury the pain. I kept myself busy, hoping to keep Grief at a distance. I was stubborn, immersed in the idea that positive thinking would be enough to carry me through. But the truth was, Grief would stand in front of Peace until I acknowledged it. I began to breathe again when I stopped running and let Grief run to me. I held open my arms and welcomed it in. Some days, it felt heavy, almost too heavy to bear, but on others, it was softer, a reminder of what I loved and lost. In those moments, I found the parts of myself I had hidden away.

Healing does not mean forgetting; it means allowing Grief to be part of your story.

You don't move on;
you just move forward.
And grief walks with you,
but so does love.
And somehow,
you find you can carry both.

There was so much pressure to convince everyone around me that I was doing well. That I was strong and courageous and resilient, and that I didn't need help. I *was* strong, I *was* courageous and resilient, too, but I *did* need help. I needed arms to wrap me tightly into a hug; I needed shoulders to lean on, ears to listen to me, a gentle whisper that ensured that, while it may not have seemed so then, eventually, things would settle, the sun would appear from behind the clouds, and I would be able to carry on. There was a calm that followed such realization—the ability to ask for help—for when I stopped fighting the need to pretend I was okay, it gave way for the ache to breathe, to just let it all go. Acceptance, I think, is really just healing wearing different clothes.

Grief's Gift

One morning, Grief appeared at my door. A shadow of silence, it said nothing as it handed me a small, weathered box. I stared at the box in confusion; I didn't want this. What could Grief offer that I'd ever want? But Grief left it with me. In the beginning, I tried to dispose of the box, but it would not leave. I tried to hide the box, bury it in distractions and things that made it less noticeable. I thought perhaps if I simply ignored it, then it would disappear. But every time I turned away, the box only grew heavier, its weight reminding me that it was still there. Months passed, and with them, the box changed. Sometimes, its edges were sharp; other times, they seemed to soften—still it followed me everywhere. One day, exhausted and no longer able to turn away, I sat with it. I held it for a long while, before finally daring to open it. Unexpectedly, inside were memories. There were some I had forgotten or pushed away, too painful to remember. Others were bright sunrays filtering through a forgotten window. I absorbed each one, remembering the pain and sorrow but also the comfort and happiness. The more I sifted through the memories, the more I realized that Grief's box had not been a curse but rather a gift. It held all the pieces of my life, all the moments I had chosen to carry forward. As I accepted this, the box became lighter, and I chose to carry it with me. A reminder of all that I had lost but also all that I'd gained.

I may not always have
the right words,
the ones you need to hear,
and the silence
sits between us like a feather.
But, still, I will be here.
Close enough
for you to lean on,
holding steady
until the days feel lighter.

In the space between grief and joy,
I have found a home—
it is here I understand that to exist
with one is to exist with the other.

The New Beginning

The dawn arrives, the night remade,
a breath of hope, as shadows fade.
In morning light, the world feels new,
the road ahead, a chance to bloom.

I was so afraid to begin again. I looked at myself in the mirror, and all I saw was failure. It was the bottom of the barrel, the depths of despair, complete defeat. There were so many days when I couldn't even face what had happened. But through the anxiety, the doubt, and the fear, I had to remember to breathe. I had been uncomfortable before; I had been scared and afraid, and it felt like the world was ending, but then it didn't, and the sun rose again. *I have survived this feeling before; I can do it again.* When you feel the anguish in your chest, heart racing, hands shaking, it blinds you to all your strength; you are sinking in that moment, but try to focus on the rise and fall of your chest. It will pass; it will always pass.

The windows will open soon,
the fresh air will fill our lungs,
there will be new songs to sing,
and colors will unfurl in the garden.

Dear March,
we begin again.

If you have ever known the loss of someone you love, then you will also know the many days and nights you have felt the deep absence of love. As though the very thing has been ripped out of your heart. This idea that all that love lived with that person, and now they're gone, as if the love vanished with them. For when you live life, you just want to share it with the person you love most; how can you live moment to moment without living it with them too? But perhaps a deeply rooted truth is that we never lose love. It is threaded into every sunset and every beautiful view. It is every drop of rain, every firefly, every star that dots the night sky. It is in our favorite books and songs and films. It is in the laughter among friends and the warmth of family. Despite how fragile life can be, and how sudden loss can feel, when you understand that love is in everything, you can take that love and share it with the world—for when it ripples out into the universe, they live on forever.

If there is a lesson I have learned, it's that I will never be able to predict life—it will always shift and change. Sometimes, it is small change, like the turning of a season, finding a new favorite café, trying a new hairstyle, or rearranging the furniture, while others alter the path I am on entirely, reshaping my world in ways I couldn't have foreseen. Grief taught me that I don't have to be everywhere all the time, that versions of me will alter and change over the years. I can embrace this uncertainty, find steadiness not in what I can control but in how I respond to it, how I let the change into my heart. Life is always unfolding, sometimes with a whisper, sometimes with a roar, and all I can do is be open to what it may bring.

Your birthday still comes every year,
and while you're not getting any older,
I like to celebrate—to pause and remember,
to honor the way you filled the world.

I set aside the day as if you were here,
light a candle, sit with your stories,
let myself feel the light and warmth
of all the lessons you left behind.

This day is still yours. A constant reminder
that love endures through time and space—
that to know you is to remember you,
to never forget you are woven into
every heartbeat and every breath.

Dear Me,

I know it feels like everything is ending right now. The loss is pressing down, heavy and relentless on your heart. Grief feels so big some days, you fear it might swallow you whole. You're looking for answers, but there are none. You're wondering if this hollow ache will be with you forever. I wish I could reach through time and tell you everything you are going to learn. I wish I could show you how much you are going to make it through, even if, right now, it's impossible to feel this way, to see the light at the end of the tunnel; but you will, and you'll be changed.

Here are the things I want you to know:

You are allowed to take things one day at a time. Some days, you might not even get out of bed, and this is okay. You don't have to move mountains every day. Sometimes, surviving means knowing a deep breath is enough.

Grief is not a straight line. It will come in waves; some will crash harder than others, but it is important to feel each one. Healing does not mean the absence of grief but learning to walk the shore alongside it.

Letting go doesn't mean forgetting. You will find ways to continue honoring what has gone, to keep a memory alive that brings you comfort instead of pain.

These memories will begin to feel like soft whispers over time, reminders that love lives on with you.

You're allowed to ask for help. You don't have to carry your grief alone. Lean on those who care for you. Strength does not lie in pretending but rather in honesty. There is nothing weak about vulnerability or asking for help.

Your heart will open again. It will feel almost impossible to pick up all the pieces of your shattered heart. For how will they all glue back together in the same way? But the truth is, the more you open yourself to love again, the more those pieces are handed back to you, never glued together the same, but they will make space for the new.

It is natural to change because of your grief. Profound loss, trauma, and grief impact us deeply. They completely reshape us. You will emerge on the other side with new boundaries, new perspectives, and new values. Embrace this change; it is how you honor your experiences.

I know you can't see it now, but one day, this will be another chapter in your story. Painful as it may be now, you're going to be proud and grateful of the new self that emerges. Someone who knows the depths of loss but also the beauty of resilience. You will never be alone, not even in this dark place.

I'm here, waiting for you with open arms and a heart that is full once more.

With all the love and strength you don't yet know you have,

The You That Survived

There were many days when I found myself retracing our steps along the trail we used to hike. Toward the center of the woods, beneath a canopy of intertwined branches, where the only sounds were the trees breathing and the birds trilling, there was a giant firewood tree, its trunk gnarled with ancient wisdom, rings holding centuries of secrets, a story written by time itself. Beneath its vast, reaching arms, I felt small but held, as if the tree understood loss and renewal better than I ever could. It was here that I met Grief and Hope. Grief sat with me in the quiet, unafraid of my tears, while Hope stood just beyond the shadows, waiting for me to notice the light breaking through the leaves.

Grief said to me, "I know you didn't expect me, didn't ask for me in any way. I came all at once, unavoidable. I hold all your pain, all the memories that feel too sharp to touch. I am a reminder of what you miss. I know it feels heavy, but the weight keeps you close to what you lost."

And Hope added, "Yes, Grief keeps you grounded in what is gone, but I am here to remind you what is still to come."

"You're so soft, Hope," Grief said. "I don't always understand you. How can you ask for beginnings when the past feels so real? I preserve the past through longing."

"I don't erase the past," Hope replied. "I honor it."

"So, I don't have to be everything? All-consuming?" Grief asked, and Hope shook its head. "You don't have to be everything. A part of a journey, an important piece, but you can rest. I will hold them steady, even when they feel small."

"Then what am I if I linger in the quiet moments and you draw them forward, one day at a time?"

"It doesn't have to be one or the other," Hope said. "We can both occupy the space."

And I looked from Grief to Hope and held out each of my hands. "Perhaps," I said softly, "we can all walk together."

The firsts that mark the beginning of a new chapter will often come quietly, almost unexpectedly. The first laugh that feels like a forgotten song, a reminder that joy isn't gone; patient and steady, it has just been waiting for a moment to return. The first sunny day, when the light streams through your window, warming you in a way that you haven't felt in so long. It is as if the world is inviting you back into the rhythm of the everyday. It is saying, "We have been waiting here the whole time." The first memory without pain, a moment of reflection, when even though it still aches, it doesn't feel as though it is breaking your heart into a million pieces. You realize that grief doesn't erase love; it transforms it. The first holiday without tears, the first cup of hot chocolate that tastes sweet again, the first time you hear a song and feel like dancing—all of those moments do not erase what you have been through, but they remind you of what is still possible. A new beginning is really the start of your changed relationship with sorrow, a reminder that you can miss someone but still live.

The quiet pause before midnight,
the in-between of what is ending
and what is waiting to begin—

a promise that perhaps things will
be better this year.

New beginnings are often on the other side of weathered bridges. Hope lives here too. And so often through life, you will stand at the foot of this bridge, its planks creaking with the weight of what once was, and you'll wonder how you are ever going to cross. But then the past settles like mist over the water below, and you take the first step. And then the next. And while the bridge stretches into the unknown, its destination unclear, with every step you take, you leave behind what cannot follow and instead move closer and closer toward embracing what will become.

To open your heart again
is to risk the ache.
Tearing down your walls,
and peeling back the layers,
is to have your soul exposed.

It is not weakness
but rather courage,
a strength that says,
"I am not what happened."

Your vulnerability opens a door
to begin again.

Accepting the things that happened
can feel like letting go of control,
stepping into the unknown.

But it is also
a reclamation of self,
choosing to believe
that life can hold beauty
even after it's been broken.

The universe reminds us
how beginnings can be soft—
like when the first light of dawn
kisses the stillness of the sea.

And perhaps if you listen closely,
you will hear the stars as they whisper
that every ending holds a seed,
for even after the fire clears the forest,
new life will always find a way.

And suddenly it's a feeling in your heart—it's time to start again and trust the process. To take that first leap, even if it's small, even if you feel uncertain. The hardest lesson is understanding the difference between moving on and moving forward. Moving forward means carrying the memory of what you have lost, holding it without letting it control how you choose to live the rest of your life. And maybe your new beginning will be about learning who you are now, from this moment forward, shaped but not defined by your past. Or maybe it will be about opening your heart again, finding someone to share your new chapters with. Whatever it may be, I hope you step into your renewal with hope, to trust that life still has so many beautiful things to offer and that you have the strength to see it through.

It's okay if you are still healing,
if the stitches of your heart
are tender and uneven.
If the bad days
are still woven into the good,
a shadow trailing the light.

It's okay to feel lost and afraid,
to wander without answers,
to carry questions
that seem impossible to answer.

Healing isn't a clear path;
it twists and loops and lingers.

But the point of it all
is to keep moving,
to keep breathing and becoming—
that is enough.

As you get older, you become more aware of what it means to start again. You know what it feels like to forgive and to be forgiven, how second chances don't always come around. You take note of the way others make you feel, the spaces you belong in, the moments that make you feel alive. You embrace simplicity—there's just something magnetic about slowing down, cooking your favorite meal, an afternoon walk, a conversation in which you are heard and seen. Chaos now feels exhausting and overwhelming. You realize that so many of us carry unseen struggles. Perhaps it is kinder to listen more, check in, give a hug that lasts a little longer, send the "Thinking of you" text, answer the call. How life feels will always matter more than how it looks. All the things you think you wanted won't always fit. They will change. And suddenly you learn to let go of the expectations, embrace the beautiful sunset instead of rushing past it. Life isn't about chasing; it's about noticing. And in the noticing, you'll find so much more peace than you ever imagined.

Is it an ending or a new beginning—
a question as old as time itself.

When things end, we mourn them,
and then, to carry forward, we must
embrace new things.

There will always be a storm that
disrupts your journey, and it will
shatter you in ways you never expected.

But the things that lie ahead
are not to be feared;
they are possibilities waiting,
asking only that you believe in them.

They are the start of something,
not the end of everything.

It was a gradual process, the introduction to the new version of me. Starting again does not happen overnight, but it also isn't impossible. The loss transformed many corners of my life, but it also gave me new perspective—I set boundaries, learned to protect my energy, to choose where I invested my heart and to whom and what I dedicated my time. I stopped trying to be everything to everyone. I started listening to myself more, that small voice deep within, the one I had spent so long ignoring. I allowed myself the space to feel, to let go, and to rebuild with intention. I understood that not every door I opened needed to be walked through, that saying no was showing kindness to myself, as I set about learning the new me. Life is a fleeting thing; there are many temporaries, but the constant is yourself. Moving forward is not a destination; it is a new way of living.

We learned to rebuild,
lyric by lyric,
an old song sung in a new key.
Familiar, yet changed,
a melody of what was,
a harmony of what had come to be.

Yes, I closed the door many times.
I was full of hurt, exhausted, angry
at what the world had taken from me.

Time and time again, I closed that door,
and I remained in the darkness—
eager to stay in the stillness and quiet.

But each day, the light was clearly visible
through the crack.

It did not matter how many times I closed
myself off; the light would always appear.

Hope will always find us,
even if we insist on sitting in darkness.

It felt like a setback, like all those years had been wasted. Everywhere I looked, I saw others moving forward—careers advancing, families growing, dreams coming true. And there I was, falling apart and having to start all over again. I was older now, and there were dreams I'd once imagined weaving into my life that seemed further away than ever, as if I'd missed my chance. It felt like time was slipping away. It was too late to hope for more, to want all those things too. But I was wrong.

The truth is that it's hardly ever about where you've been but rather where you are going next. All those years, those choices, they had not been a waste. They shape us, adding layers and complexities that make us who we are. So often, we become so tangled in the idea of a perfect time line that we forget life is not a script. We cannot erase the things that have happened to us; all we can do is grow from them. Perhaps life looks different from how you had imagined, but you are still here, still living, and you can create a life that fills you with joy, and love, and purpose.

It's never too late.

In my house, grief and hope
live side by side.
Two strangers that found
a home in my heart.

Grief, with its heavy hands,
teaches me what it means to feel.
Hope, soft and stubborn,
grows like wildflowers in
all the forgotten places—
whispering, *Still, still we heal.*

There is no fight for space,
no argument on who comes first.
Instead, I always find them entwined.
Part of me, equal worth.

One reminds me of what I've lost,
and the other what I still have to find.

Life as I had known it ended one day—abruptly. It all came crashing down in a single instant. I had closed my eyes, and as I dreamed, my soul was still my soul, but then I awoke, and I had been irreversibly changed. With this new becoming, a grief arrived that I had never expected, a hollow nothingness that shattered all that I had been to pieces. My heart was filled with an ache that seemed to last an eternity. As it happened, a new road appeared before me. It spoke to me in soft sunlight and warm skies. It whispered of a new way to be. I was fearful: Who would I be along this new path? Where would I go? What would I do? And that was the point. I was lost, but change would find me again. My heart unfurled in the moment I met you, and I understood second chances.

The world is softer because you're here.
I hope you know that.
May you find peace in the simple things—
a hug that feels safe,
a hand that stays,
a story that helps you breathe again,
the sky changing colors just to remind you,
all things pass.

May you strengthen in what you've lost,
with courage and persistence.
Always knowing that love is wrapped
around you like the morning sun.

You are everything that is on their way,
everything just beginning.

On a tree branch, outside my window,
a raven perched, eyes glinting
like the shadows in the night.
It reminded me of all the days
I thought would never end—
grief is a heavy weight.
A suffocating quiet.

I would watch the raven, wings like a cloak.
It echoed emptiness, a reminder of loss,
a picture of endings.

And then one day, a bluebird came—
tentative and bright.
A song of something new to come.
A hint of sun after years of rain,
a promise to start again.

It took all that I was becoming to break free
from the dark and the lingering shadows.
The raven had such a grip.
But I learned to listen to the bluebird's song,
to allow it into my heart.

Now, I see them both, the raven, and the bluebird.
Two sides entwined together—death and life.

For neither exists without the other;
and in their contrast, I find my strength.
The raven still comes, its presence part of me,
but the bluebird's song is louder now—
I live with both.

Winnie's Lesson

This is what I always want you to know—

Grief, I have learned, is a relentless tide. It comes and goes with the moon. And yet, I have found strength is much the same. How wonderful that even in sorrow, there is space for joy.

You must embrace your quirks, your whoopsie doos, your over-the-top, out-there everything-ness. For in our quirks lie our sparks for life. Cherish the unexpected paths—they lead to the most wondrous adventures.

Loss is not an end, but something new. Even if it fills you with despair, dread, and heartache, you must unearth these things, understand there is transformation in between.

Love deeply, without reservation. Love the people you care about, fall in love, forgive when forgiveness is needed. Forgive yourself often, even if it is difficult.

Dance—in the rain, in the living room, in the middle of the kitchen. Dance with your friends, throw your hands up and shake all the worry from your body. These are small moments that will never be returned to you. Hold them, so that the memory lives on forever.

Poetry is a lighthouse. When the nights feel too long, read until you find your way again.

Be kind, especially to yourself, for self-compassion is the root of all healing. When you are kind to yourself, you are kind to others.

Hope is stubborn—keep it that way. Even on the days when it feels foolish to believe, believe anyway.

Live, even when it's messy. *Especially* when it's messy.

That's where you'll find yourself.

To the grief group that lived in my head and is now out in the world, Misery Loves Company. Misery loves company, sure, but so does hope and healing.

Additional Resources

Thank you for reading this book. Grief and loss are profound experiences, and if any of the topics discussed here have impacted you, please know that support is available. You are not alone in your journey. If you find yourself needing help, reach out to one of the following organizations for guidance, counseling, or just a listening ear:

UNITED STATES:
Dougy Center – www.dougy.org
Grief in Common – www.griefincommon.com
GriefShare – www.griefshare.org

UNITED KINGDOM:
AtaLoss – www.ataloss.org
The Good Grief Trust – www.thegoodgrieftrust.org
Winstons Wish (children, teenagers, young adults) – www.winstonswish.org

AUSTRALIA:
Beyond Blue – www.beyondblue.org.au
The Compassionate Friends Australia – www.tcfa.org.au
GriefLine – griefline.org.au
Headspace – www.headspace.org.au

PODCASTS:
Good Mourning – Sally Douglas and Imogen Carn
The Grief Coach – Brooke James
The Grief Gang – Amber Jeffrey

Remember, you don't have to navigate this path alone—there are people and resources ready to help you.

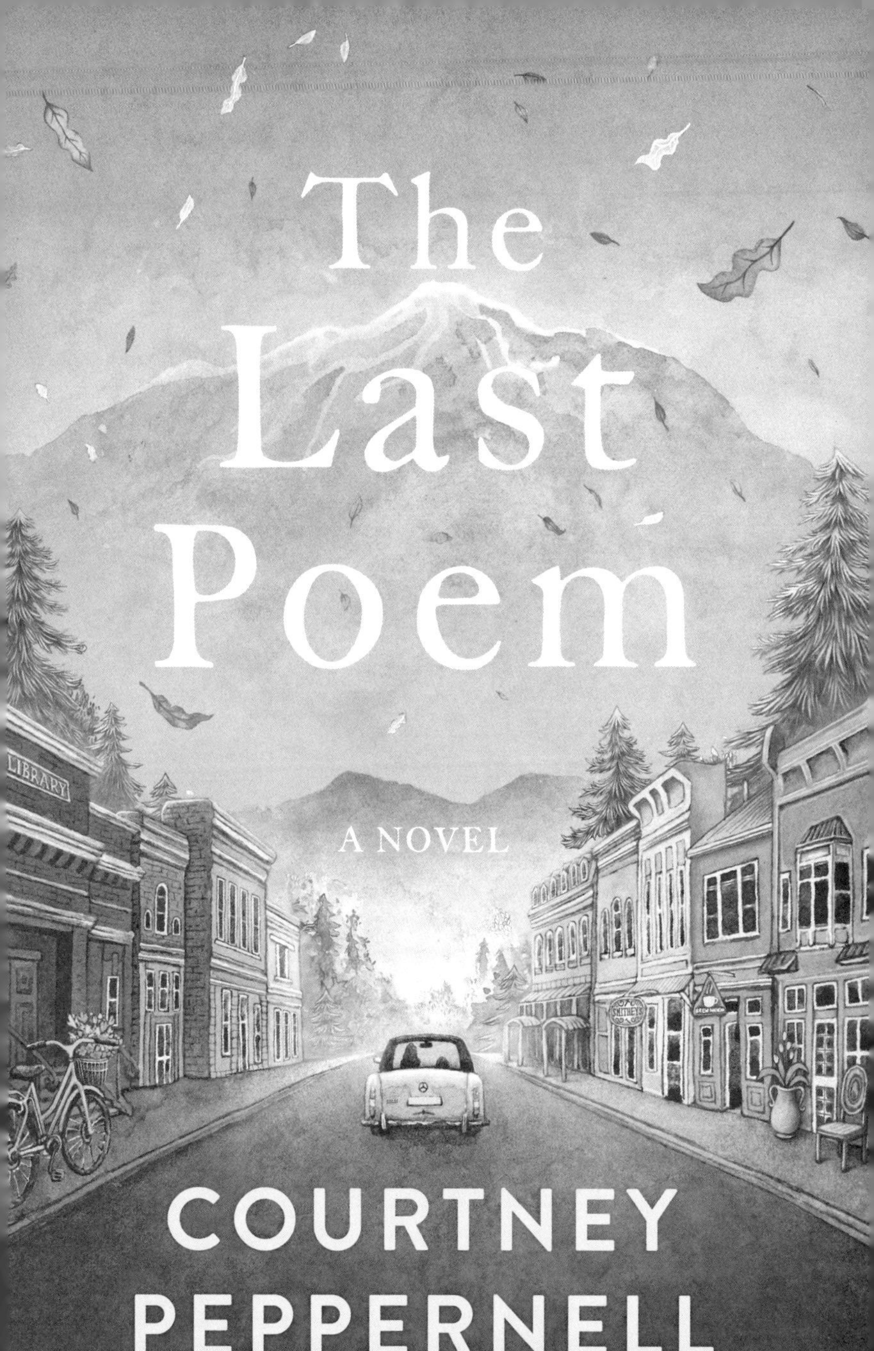

The Last Poem

A NOVEL

COURTNEY PEPPERNELL

INTERNATIONAL BESTSELLING AUTHOR OF *PILLOW THOUGHTS*

The authorised representative in the EEA is Simon and Schuster Netherlands BV, Herculesplein 96 3584 AA Utrecht, Netherlands. (info@simonandschuster.nl)

Andrews McMeel Publishing
a division of Andrews McMeel Universal
1130 Walnut Street, Kansas City, Missouri 64106
www.andrewsmcmeel.com

26 27 28 29 30 TEN 10 9 8 7 6 5 4 3 2 1

ISBN: 978-1-5248-8675-2

Library of Congress Control Number: 2026932348

Editor: Danys Mares
Art Director: Diane Marsh
Production Editor: Elizabeth A. Garcia
Production Manager: Julie Skalla

FSC
www.fsc.org
MIX
Paper | Supporting responsible forestry
FSC® C016973